July 2014

REGULATORY IMPACT ANALYSIS

Development of Social Cost of Carbon Estimates

GAO-14-663

GAO Highlights

Highlights of GAO-14-663, a report to congressional requesters

REGULATORY IMPACT ANALYSIS

Development of Social Cost of Carbon Estimates

Why GAO Did This Study

Executive Order 12866 directs federal agencies to assess the economic effects of their proposed significant regulatory actions, including a determination that a regulation's benefits justify the costs. In 2008, a federal appeals court directed DOT to update a regulatory impact analysis with an estimate of the social cost of carbon—the dollar value of the net effects (damages and benefits) of an increase in emissions of carbon dioxide, a greenhouse gas.

In 2009, the Interagency Working Group on Social Cost of Carbon was convened to develop estimates for use governmentwide, and it issued final estimates in its 2010 Technical Support Document. In 2013, the group issued revised estimates that were about 50 percent higher than the 2010 estimates, which raised public interest.

GAO was asked to review the working group's development of social cost of carbon estimates. This report describes the participating entities and processes and methods they used to develop the 2010 and 2013 estimates. GAO reviewed executive orders, OMB guidance, the Technical Support Document, its 2013 update, and other key documents. GAO interviewed officials who participated in the working group on behalf of the EOP offices and agencies involved. GAO did not evaluate the quality of the working group's approach.

GAO is making no recommendations in this report. Of seven agencies, OMB and Treasury provided written or oral comments and generally agreed with the findings in this report. Other agencies provided technical comments only or had no comments.

View GAO-14-663. For more information, contact J. Alfredo Gómez at (202) 512-3841 or gomezj@gao.gov.

What GAO Found

To develop the 2010 and 2013 social cost of carbon estimates, the Office of Management and Budget (OMB) and Council of Economic Advisers convened and led an informal interagency working group in which four other offices from the Executive Office of the President (EOP) and six federal agencies participated. Participating agencies were the Environmental Protection Agency (EPA) and the Departments of Agriculture, Commerce, Energy, Transportation (DOT), and the Treasury. According to several working group participants, the working group included relevant subject-matter experts and the agencies likely to use the estimates in future rulemakings. According to OMB staff, there is no single approach for convening informal interagency working groups and no requirement that this type of working group should document its activities or proceedings. However, OMB and EPA participants stated that the working group documented all major issues discussed in the Technical Support Document, which is consistent with federal standards for internal control. According to the Technical Support Document and participants GAO interviewed, the working group's processes and methods reflected the following three principles:

- *Used consensus-based decision making.* The working group used a consensus-based approach for making key decisions in developing the 2010 and 2013 estimates. Participants generally stated that they were satisfied that the Technical Support Document addressed individual comments on draft versions and reflected the overall consensus of the working group.

- *Relied on existing academic literature and models.* The working group relied largely on existing academic literature and models to develop its estimates. Specifically, the working group used three prevalent academic models that integrate climate and economic data to estimate future economic effects from climate change. The group agreed on three modeling inputs reflecting the wide uncertainty in the academic literature, including discount rates. Once the group reached agreement, EPA officials—sometimes with the assistance of the model developers—calculated the estimates. All other model assumptions and features were unchanged by the working group, which weighted each model equally to calculate estimates. After the academic models were updated to reflect new scientific information, such as in sea level rise and associated damages, the working group used the updated models to revise its estimates in 2013, resulting in higher estimates.

- *Took steps to disclose limitations and incorporate new information.* The Technical Support Document discloses several limitations of the estimates and areas that the working group identified as being in need of additional research. It also sets a goal of revisiting the estimates when substantially updated models become available. Since 2008, agencies have published dozens of regulatory actions for public comment that use various social cost of carbon estimates in regulatory analyses and, according to working group participants, agencies received many comments on the estimates throughout this process. Several participants told GAO that the working group decided to revise the estimates in 2013 after a number of public comments encouraged revisions because the models used to develop the 2010 estimates had been updated and used in peer-reviewed academic literature.

_____ United States Government Accountability Office

Contents

Abbreviations

ADS-B	Automatic Dependent Surveillance-Broadcast
ATC	Air Traffic Control
DICE	Dynamic Integrated Climate and Economy
DOT	Department of Transportation
EOP	Executive Office of the President
EPA	Environmental Protection Agency
FUND	Climate Framework for Uncertainty, Negotiation, and Distribution
NHTSA	National Highway Traffic Safety Administration
OMB	Office of Management and Budget
PAGE	Policy Analysis of the Greenhouse Effect

GAO
U.S. GOVERNMENT ACCOUNTABILITY OFFICE

441 G St. N.W.
Washington, DC 20548

July 24, 2014

The Honorable David Vitter
Ranking Member
Committee on Environment and Public Works
United States Senate

The Honorable Tim Murphy
Chairman
Subcommittee on Oversight and Investigations
Committee on Energy and Commerce
House of Representatives

The Honorable John Culberson
House of Representatives

The Honorable Duncan Hunter
House of Representatives

To encourage a regulatory system that protects and improves health, safety, the environment, and the economy, without imposing unreasonable costs on society, federal agencies are required to assess the economic effects of proposed significant regulatory actions. Agencies can use regulatory impact analysis to assess whether a proposed regulation's benefits justify the costs. For example, regulations aimed at benefiting society by decreasing health risks associated with air pollution may require regulated entities, such as power plants, to incur costs for installing pollution control technologies. According to Environmental Protection Agency (EPA) officials, beginning in 2008, some agencies' regulatory impact analyses incorporated estimates of the social cost of carbon,[1] which agencies use to value the net effects of reducing or

---

[1] The social cost of carbon (measured in dollars per metric ton of carbon dioxide) is the monetized net effects (damages and benefits) associated with an incremental increase in carbon emissions in a given year. Estimates of the social cost of carbon depend on the data and the models used to calculate them and can include a wide range of damage categories, such as projected changes in net agricultural productivity, human health, and property damages from increased flood risk due to increased carbon emissions. Monetization is the process of estimating the dollar value of benefits and costs.

increasing carbon dioxide emissions.[2] In 2009, in part because agencies used varying estimates of the social cost of carbon, the Executive Office of the President's (EOP) Office of Management and Budget (OMB) and Council of Economic Advisers convened an interagency working group to develop social cost of carbon estimates for federal agencies to use in their regulatory impact analyses. The working group finalized its estimates in 2010 and included them in a document—called the Technical Support Document—that also provides guidance for agencies on using the estimates.[3] In May 2013, the working group issued an update to the Technical Support Document that included revised estimates of the social cost of carbon.[4] These 2013 estimates of the social cost of carbon were approximately 50 percent higher than the 2010 estimates, which raised public interest.

You asked us to review the interagency working group's development of social cost of carbon estimates. This report describes the approach used, including participating entities and processes and methods, to develop the 2010 and 2013 social cost of carbon estimates for regulatory impact analysis.

To address this objective, we reviewed pertinent requirements and guidance, including executive orders and OMB guidance; the Technical Support Document and its 2013 update; published materials and presentations by working group participants on the development of the social cost of carbon estimates; and related GAO reports. We interviewed current and former federal officials or staff who participated in the working group on behalf of the EOP offices and agencies named in the Technical

---

[2]Carbon dioxide is a greenhouse gas recognized as a major contributor to climate change. Concentrations of greenhouse gases—including carbon dioxide, methane, nitrous oxide, and synthetic chemicals such as fluorinated gases—trap heat in the atmosphere and prevent it from returning to space.

[3]Interagency Working Group on Social Cost of Carbon, United States Government, *Technical Support Document: Social Cost of Carbon for Regulatory Impact Analysis under Executive Order 12866* (Washington, D.C.: February 2010).

[4]Interagency Working Group on Social Cost of Carbon, United States Government, *Technical Support Document: Technical Update of the Social Cost of Carbon for Regulatory Impact Analysis under Executive Order 12866* (Washington, D.C.: May 2013). This document was reissued with minor technical corrections in November 2013.

Support Document.[5] We identified these participants by contacting all of the agencies and OMB and then following up with additional individuals identified during our discussions with them. Through this process, we interviewed over 20 individuals who participated in the working group to develop the estimates in the Technical Support Document or its 2013 update, or both. We also corresponded with researchers who developed key academic materials the working group used. Our review describes the approach the working group used to develop estimates of the social cost of carbon; evaluating the quality of the approach is outside the scope of this review.

We conducted this performance audit from November 2013 to July 2014 in accordance with generally accepted government auditing standards. Those standards require that we plan and perform the audit to obtain sufficient, appropriate evidence to provide a reasonable basis for our findings and conclusions based on our audit objectives. We believe that the evidence obtained provides a reasonable basis for our findings and conclusions based on our audit objectives.

Background

Executive Order 12866 directs federal agencies to assess the potential costs and benefits of their significant regulatory actions, consisting of several categories of regulatory actions, including those likely to result in a rule that may have an annual effect on the economy of $100 million or more or that have a material adverse effect on the economy; a sector of the economy; productivity; competition; jobs; the environment; public health or safety; or state, local, or tribal governments or communities.[6] Under the executive order, for regulatory actions expected to meet this

---

[5]According to the Technical Support Document, the working group consisted of participants from the Council of Economic Advisers, Council on Environmental Quality, EPA, National Economic Council, Office of Energy and Climate Change, OMB, Office of Science and Technology Policy, and the Departments of Agriculture, Commerce, Energy, Transportation, and the Treasury. In March 2011, the Office of Energy and Climate Change joined the Domestic Policy Council.

[6]Exec. Order No. 12866, 58 Fed. Reg. 51,735 (Sept. 30, 1993). Other significant regulatory actions include those that are likely to result in a rule that may create a serious inconsistency or otherwise interfere with an action taken or planned by another agency; materially alter the budgetary impact of entitlements, grants, user fees, or loan programs or the rights and obligations of recipients thereof; or raise novel legal or policy issues arising out of legal mandates, the President's priorities, or the principles set forth in Executive Order 12866.

threshold, or economically significant regulatory actions, agencies must also assess costs and benefits of reasonably feasible alternatives and explain why the planned regulatory action is preferable to the identified alternatives. For each significant regulatory action, the agency is to develop the proposed regulation and associated regulatory impact analysis and submit them to OMB for formal review. After OMB concludes its review, the agency is to publish the proposed rule in the *Federal Register* for public comment. The agency is to issue a document summarizing its consideration of the public comments and, if appropriate, modify the proposed rule in response to the comments. This phase of regulatory development may also include further internal and external review. For significant regulatory actions, the agency is to submit the final regulatory impact analysis and regulation to OMB for review before it publishes the final rule.

In 2003, OMB issued Circular A-4 to provide guidance to federal agencies on the development of regulatory analysis as directed by Executive Order 12866.[7] Circular A-4 states that it is designed to assist agencies by defining good regulatory analysis and standardizing the way benefits and costs of federal regulatory actions are measured and reported. In particular, the guidance provides for systematic evaluation of qualitative and quantitative benefits and costs, including their monetization. Circular A-4 also provides guidance on the selection of discount rates to adjust the estimated benefits and costs for differences in timing.[8] According to Circular A-4, a regulatory impact analysis should include an evaluation of the benefits and costs of the proposed action and any reasonable alternatives, as well as a description of assumptions and uncertainty.[9] It acknowledges that agencies cannot analyze all regulations according to a

---

[7]OMB, Circular A-4: Regulatory Analysis (Sept. 17, 2003).

[8]When the benefits and costs of a regulatory action will occur in the future, agencies must determine the present value of future benefits and costs by applying an appropriate discount rate—the interest rate used to convert benefits and costs occurring in different time periods to a common present value.

[9]Circular A-4 states that agencies should discount future benefits and costs using rates of 3 and 7 percent but notes that agencies may, in addition, consider a lower discount rate if a rule will have important intergenerational benefits or costs. In July 2014, we reported on the application of the guidance in Circular A-4 and the Technical Support Document and made recommendations to OMB to help clarify the relationship between those two documents. See GAO, *Environmental Regulation: EPA Should Improve Adherence to Guidance for Selected Elements of Regulatory Impact Analyses*, GAO-14-519 (Washington, D.C.: July 18, 2014).

formula, and that different regulations may call for different emphases in the analysis. Executive Order 13563, which reaffirmed and supplemented Executive Order 12866 in 2011, generally directs federal agencies to conduct regulatory actions based on the best available science.[10] It also directs agencies to use the best available techniques to quantify benefits and costs accurately.

Federal agencies began including estimates of the social cost of carbon in regulatory impact analyses following a decision by the U.S. Court of Appeals for the Ninth Circuit. Specifically, in 2006, the Department of Transportation's National Highway Traffic Safety Administration (NHTSA) issued a final rule on fuel economy standards for certain vehicles which, like other regulations at the time, did not include estimates of the social cost of carbon.[11] The final rule stated that the agency had identified a benefit from a significant reduction in carbon dioxide emissions but stated that the dollar value of the benefit could not be determined because of the wide variation in published estimates of the social cost of carbon. In 2008, in response to a challenge from 11 states and several other organizations, the Ninth Circuit held that NHTSA had acted arbitrarily and capriciously by failing to monetize the value of carbon emissions reduction and directed NHTSA to include such a monetized value in an updated regulatory impact analysis for the regulation.[12] The court stated that, "[w]hile the record shows that there is a range of values, the value of carbon emissions reduction is certainly not zero."[13] Following the court's decision, the Department of Energy, the Department of Transportation, and EPA incorporated a variety of individually developed estimates of the social cost of carbon into their regulatory analyses. These estimates were derived from academic literature and ranged, in general, from $0 to $159 (in 2006, 2007, or 2008 dollars) per metric ton of carbon dioxide emitted

---

[10]Exec. Order No. 13563, 76 Fed. Reg. 3821 (Jan. 18, 2011).

[11]Average Fuel Economy Standards for Light Trucks Model Years 2008-2011, 71 Fed. Reg. 17,566 (Apr. 6, 2006). According to EPA officials, other regulations at the time did not typically quantify changes in carbon emissions.

[12]*Ctr. For Biological Diversity v. Nat'l Highway Traffic Safety Admin.*, 538 F.3d 1172, 1203 (9th Cir. 2008). The Ninth Circuit issued the 2008 opinion after vacating and withdrawing its prior opinion, 508 F.3d 508, issued on Nov. 15, 2007.

[13]*Id.* at 1200.

GAO-14-663 Social Cost of Carbon

in 2007. They also varied in whether they reflected domestic or global measures of the social cost of carbon.[14]

In early 2009, in part to improve consistency in agencies' use of social cost of carbon estimates for regulatory impact analysis, OMB's Office of Information and Regulatory Affairs and the Council of Economic Advisers convened the Interagency Working Group on Social Cost of Carbon. The working group developed interim governmentwide social cost of carbon estimates based on an average of selected estimates published in academic literature. The interim estimates first appeared—and, thus, were first available for public review—in August 2009 in the Department of Energy's final rule on energy standards for vending machines.[15] Agencies subsequently incorporated the interim estimates into several published regulatory actions that sought public comments to inform the development of final estimates for future use. The middle or "central" value for the range of interim estimates was $19 (in 2006 dollars) per metric ton of carbon dioxide emitted in 2007.[16]

In October 2009, after developing the interim estimates, the working group reassembled to begin developing the final social cost of carbon estimates issued in the Technical Support Document. While the Technical Support Document is dated February 2010, it was first released publicly in March 2010 as an appendix to the Department of Energy's final rule on energy standards for small electric motors.[17] Subsequently, dozens of published regulatory actions incorporated the estimates. The Technical

---

[14]The benefits and costs of reducing most greenhouse gas emissions, including carbon dioxide, differ from most other benefits and costs in at least two respects: (1) greenhouse gas emissions can contribute to global damages even when emitted in the United States because these emissions can disperse widely throughout the atmosphere, and (2) these emissions generally remain in the atmosphere for years, causing subsequent long-term damages. While Circular A-4 states that agencies should generally estimate domestic benefits and costs of regulations, it also provides latitude to include global economic effects resulting from regulations when relevant and states that such effects should be reported separately and in addition to domestic effects.

[15]Energy Conservation Program: Energy Conservation Standards for Refrigerated Bottled or Canned Beverage Vending Machines, 74 Fed. Reg. 44,914 (Aug. 31, 2009).

[16]The working group calculated five interim estimates of the social cost of carbon using different discount rate scenarios and referred to $19—the middle of the five estimates—as the "central value."

[17]Energy Conservation Program: Energy Conservation Standards for Small Electric Motors, 75 Fed. Reg. 10,874 (Mar. 9, 2010).

GAO-14-663 Social Cost of Carbon

Support Document states that the working group agreed to regularly update the social cost of carbon estimates as the research underlying the estimates evolves. In June 2013, after using the 2010 estimates in an earlier proposal of the rule, the Department of Energy's final rule on energy standards for microwaves was the first regulatory action to incorporate the revised estimates developed by the working group in the 2013 update to the Technical Support Document.[18] Table 1 shows the central values for the range of 2010 and 2013 social cost of carbon estimates for carbon emissions occurring in selected years.

Table 1: Central Values for the Social Cost of Carbon Estimates Issued by the Interagency Working Group on Social Cost of Carbon in 2010 and 2013

Dollars are 2007 dollars per metric ton of carbon dioxide

Year	2010 central values	2013 central values
2010	$21	$32
2020	26	43
2030	33	52
2040	39	61
2050	$45	$71

Source: Interagency Working Group on Social Cost of Carbon's Technical Support Document and 2013 update. | GAO-14-663

Note: The Technical Support Document states that the working group calculated the social cost of carbon for emissions occurring in multiple future years to cover the time horizons anticipated for upcoming regulatory analysis. When the benefits and costs of a regulatory action will occur in the future, agencies must determine the present value of future benefits and costs by applying an appropriate discount rate—the interest rate used to convert benefits and costs occurring in different periods to a common present value. According to the Technical Support Document, the social cost of carbon estimates increase over time because future emissions are expected to produce larger incremental damages as the environment and the economy become more stressed in response to greater climate change. The working group selected four values of the social cost of carbon for regulatory analysis. The first three values are based on the average of estimates calculated at discount rates of 2.5 percent, 3 percent, and 5 percent, and the fourth value was included to represent higher-than-expected economic impacts at the 3 percent discount rate. The Technical Support Document refers to the average of estimates calculated at the 3 percent discount rate as the "central value" of the social cost of carbon and states that agencies should consider all four values when conducting regulatory analyses.

Appendix I lists regulatory actions from 2008 to 2014 and the type of social cost of carbon estimates (i.e., individually developed, interim, 2010, or 2013) incorporated in the actions' regulatory analyses.

---

[18]Energy Conservation Program: Energy Conservation Standards for Standby Mode and Off Mode for Microwave Ovens, 78 Fed. Reg. 36,316 (June 17, 2013).

Approach Used to Develop Estimates of the Social Cost of Carbon

According to the Technical Support Document and participants we interviewed, the working group consisted of participants representing six EOP offices and six federal agencies and was convened under Executive Order 12866. The working group's processes and methods for developing the estimates reflected three key principles. Specifically, according to participants, the working group (1) used consensus-based decision making; (2) relied largely on existing academic literature and models, including technical assistance from outside resources; and (3) took steps to disclose limitations and incorporate new information by considering public comments and revising the estimates as updated research became available.

Participating Entities

According to the Technical Support Document and participants we spoke with, OMB and the Council of Economic Advisers convened and led the working group, and four other EOP offices and six federal agencies actively participated in the group. According to several participants, the participating EOP offices included the relevant subject-matter experts to best contribute on behalf of the EOP,[19] and the other participating agencies were those likely to conduct rulemakings affecting carbon emissions and, therefore, use the social cost of carbon estimates in the future. For example, EPA and the Department of Energy have issued numerous rules using the social cost of carbon estimates (see app. I).

OMB staff and EPA officials told us that OMB and the Council of Economic Advisers decided which EOP offices and federal agencies to invite to participate in the working group and, according to participants we interviewed from several agencies, each agency that chose to participate decided which of its internal offices would send representatives. OMB staff stated that any federal agency was welcome to participate in the working group, and EPA officials told us that at least two invited agencies declined to participate. OMB staff recalled that the working group generally included up to several participants from each participating office and agency and numbered approximately two dozen participants in total.

---

[19]We previously reported that four of these EOP offices—the Council on Environmental Quality, Office of Energy and Climate Change, OMB, and Office of Science and Technology Policy—provide high-level policy direction for federal climate change programs and activities and commonly lead formal and informal interagency initiatives on related issues. See GAO, *Climate Change: Improvements Needed to Clarify National Priorities and Better Align Them with Federal Funding Decisions*, GAO-11-317 (Washington, D.C.: May 20, 2011).

Table 2 lists the 12 participating offices and agencies, along with the internal offices they sent to represent them on the working group.

Table 2: Offices and Agencies Participating in the Interagency Working Group on Social Cost of Carbon to Develop the 2010 and 2013 Social Cost of Carbon Estimates

	Participating office or agency	2010 estimates	2013 estimates
Executive Office of the President			
	Council of Economic Advisers[a]	X	X
	Council on Environmental Quality	X	X
	National Economic Council	X	X
	Office of Energy and Climate Change[b]	X	X
	Office of Management and Budget[a] Office of Information and Regulatory Affairs	X	X
	Office of Science and Technology Policy	X	X
Federal agencies			
	Department of Agriculture		
	• Office of the Chief Economist	X	X
	Department of Commerce[c]		
	• International Trade Administration, Office of Competition and Economic Analysis[d]	X	
	• National Oceanic and Atmospheric Administration, National Marine Fisheries Service[e]		X
	Department of Energy[f]		
	• Office of Climate Change Policy and Technology[g]	X	X
	Department of Transportation		
	• Office of the Secretary	X	X
	• Volpe, The National Transportation Systems Center	X	
	Department of the Treasury		
	• Office of Economic Policy	X	
	• Office of International Affairs, Office of Environment and Energy	X	X
	Environmental Protection Agency		
	• Office of Air and Radiation, Office of Atmospheric Programs	X	X
	• Office of Policy, National Center for Environmental Economics	X	X

Source: GAO analysis of information provided by the Office of Management and Budget, Environmental Protection Agency, and Departments of Agriculture, Commerce, Energy, Transportation, and the Treasury. | GAO-14-663

[a]The Council of Economic Advisers and the Office of Management and Budget convened and led the working group to develop the 2010 and 2013 estimates.

[b]In March 2011, the Office of Energy and Climate Change joined the Domestic Policy Council.

In establishing the working group, several participants told us that OMB and the Council of Economic Advisers made efforts to ensure that the group's members, collectively, brought the necessary technical expertise for developing social cost of carbon estimates. For example, according to these participants and EPA documentation, participants from the EOP offices included individuals with expertise in pertinent topics, such as economics and climate science. The former Deputy Assistant Secretary for Environment and Energy at the Department of the Treasury stated that he was invited to participate in the working group because of his prior experience researching ways to discount costs and benefits across generations. In addition, the former Administrator of the Energy Information Administration told us that he was asked to participate, in part, based on his previous experience evaluating climate models while conducting research with the National Academy of Sciences. According to an OMB staff member, the six participating federal agencies were also responsible for ensuring that they provided adequate technical expertise to the working group. Agency representatives included environmental economists and climate scientists, among other key professionals. According to EPA documentation, participants from EPA also provided technical expertise in climate science, economics, and academic modeling to the broader group, as needed.

When the working group reconvened in 2013 to update the estimates, the same EOP offices and agencies generally participated, although some of the individuals participating on behalf of offices or agencies changed, in part due to individuals changing positions or leaving the government altogether. Also, some participants who previously had been serving details at other participating agencies had returned to their home agencies. For example, certain participants who were on detail to the

Council of Economic Advisers during the development of the 2010 Technical Support Document instead represented EPA on the working group during the development of the 2013 update.

According to the Technical Support Document, the working group was convened under the broad direction of Executive Order 12866 for agencies to assess the costs and benefits of intended regulations.[20] In addition, participants from several agencies told us that the executive order was the key requirement driving the working group's effort to develop social cost of carbon estimates. OMB staff stated that, while there is no single requirement or other approach for convening interagency working groups, it is appropriate for OMB to form interagency working groups to collaborate on policy or analytic needs identified under Executive Order 12866. These OMB staff members said that, instead of being organized under a written agreement or other requirements, the working group was an informal interagency working group with no charter or other convening document. According to OMB staff, there was no requirement that the informal working group should document its activities or proceedings, including the meetings held or specific discussions that occurred at each. However, OMB staff and EPA officials stated that all major issues discussed during working group meetings are documented in the Technical Support Document and its 2013 update, which is consistent with the control activities standard in the federal standards for internal control.[21] We have also reported that interagency working groups use a variety of mechanisms to implement interagency collaborative efforts, including temporary working groups,[22] and that not all collaborative arrangements, particularly those that are informal, need to be documented through written guidance and agreements.[23]

---

[20]The 2013 update to the Technical Support Document adds that Executive Order 13563, issued after the working group developed the 2010 social cost of carbon estimates, commits the administration to regulatory decision making based on the best available science.

[21]GAO, *Standards for Internal Control in the Federal Government*, GAO/AIMD-00-21.3.1 (Washington, D.C.: November 1999).

[22]GAO, GAO-11-317; *Managing for Results: Key Considerations for Implementing Interagency Collaborative Mechanisms*, GAO-12-1022 (Washington, D.C.: Sept. 27, 2012); and *Managing for Results: Implementation Approaches Used to Enhance Collaboration in Interagency Groups*, GAO-14-220 (Washington, D.C.: Feb. 14, 2014).

[23]GAO-12-1022.

Processes and Methods

Participants told us that the working group's processes and methods reflected three key principles. First, the group used consensus-based decision making. Second, the group relied largely on existing academic literature and models, including technical assistance from outside resources. Third, the group took steps to disclose limitations and incorporate new information by considering public comments and revising the estimates as updated research became available.

Used Consensus-Based Decision Making

All of the participants we spoke with said that the working group used a consensus-based approach for making key decisions on developing the social cost of carbon estimates. Most participants said that the working group's overall approach was open and collegial, and that participants had many opportunities to make contributions and raise issues for discussion that were important to them.

OMB staff stated that the working group did not assign roles or responsibilities, and many participants told us that different working group participants and agencies volunteered to take responsibility for various aspects of the development of the estimates that fell within their particular areas of expertise. For example, OMB staff stated that, while OMB and the Council of Economic Advisers were the official leaders of the working group meetings, all EOP offices that participated played a large role during the meetings, and discussions were informal. According to these staff and other officials we spoke with, participants could generally choose the extent of their involvement, and all participants' contributions were considered equally.

According to many participants, the Council of Economic Advisers coordinated drafting the Technical Support Document, including gathering feedback from working group members. Specifically, they told us that, following the meetings, officials from the Council of Economic Advisers summarized the group discussions to include in the latest draft of the Technical Support Document and circulated draft sections of the Technical Support Document for the working group to review. For example, a participant told us that he raised concerns about whether the Technical Support Document provided adequate information on domestic measures of the social cost of carbon. The participant said that, in response to this feedback, the working group decided to include a separate discussion in the Technical Support Document on estimating domestic benefits and costs. The Technical Support Document states that reported domestic effects should be calculated using a range of values from 7 to 23 percent of the global measure of the social cost of carbon, although it cautions that these values are approximate, provisional, and highly speculative due to limited evidence. None of the participants we spoke with expressed concerns about how their contributions were incorporated into the final Technical Support Document. The participants generally stated that they were satisfied that the final Technical Support Document successfully addressed individual comments on the draft version and the overall consensus of the working group and its participating offices and agencies.

Relied on Existing Academic Literature and Models

The Technical Support Document states that the main objective of the working group was to develop a range of estimates of the social cost of carbon using a defensible set of modeling inputs based on existing academic literature. Many participants confirmed that the working group relied largely on existing academic literature and models to develop its estimates. According to the Technical Support Document and many participants we spoke with, the working group calculated its estimates using three models that integrate climate and economic data into a single modeling framework for estimating future economic effects resulting from climate change.[24] In general, each model translates carbon dioxide emissions scenarios into changes in greenhouse gas concentrations in the atmosphere, greenhouse gas concentrations in the atmosphere into temperature changes, and temperature changes into net economic effects (i.e., damages and benefits). However, each model uses its own methods to estimate these effects. The Technical Support Document states that the three models are frequently cited in peer-reviewed literature. They have also been used in climate assessments by the Intergovernmental Panel on Climate Change—an organization within the United Nations that assesses scientific, technical, and economic information on the effects of climate change. In addition, the National Research Council of the National Academies recognized these three models as three of the most widely used models of their kind.[25]

Many participants told us that the working group spent most of its meeting time reviewing and discussing academic literature to help decide on

---

[24]The three models are Dynamic Integrated Climate and Economy (DICE), Climate Framework for Uncertainty, Negotiation, and Distribution (FUND), and Policy Analysis of the Greenhouse Effect (PAGE). They were first developed in the early 1990s by researchers acknowledged as leaders in their field and are updated regularly based on new developments in climate and economic research.

[25]National Research Council, *Hidden Costs of Energy: Unpriced Consequences of Energy Production and Use* (Washington, D.C.: National Academies Press, 2010).

GAO-14-663 Social Cost of Carbon

values for three key modeling inputs to run in each model. The key modeling inputs the working group selected were based on data from prevalent research organizations, such as the Stanford Energy Modeling Forum, and reflected the wide uncertainty in the academic literature, according to the Technical Support Document.[26] These inputs were as follows:

- scenarios for future population and economic growth (i.e., gross domestic product) and carbon dioxide emissions,
- a measure of the climate's responsiveness to increased concentrations of greenhouse gases in the atmosphere—known as equilibrium climate sensitivity,[27] and
- discount rates.

Several participants told us that different meetings focused on different modeling inputs and included technical presentations by participants with expertise in each technical area. For example, due to their previous experience working with the models, EPA officials made presentations on how each model works. OMB staff stated that the technical presentations focused on the academic materials cited in the Technical Support Document, including dozens of peer-reviewed journal articles. They also said that all technical decisions discussed in the Technical Support Document were arrived at by consensus through this process. Several participants said that a significant amount of the group's discussions focused on selecting discount rates that best reflect the most current academic literature, while also comporting with OMB's guidance in Circular A-4. The Technical Support Document cites guidance from Circular A-4 in its discussion of many technical topics, including its selection of discount rates. It states that the discount rate (i.e., 3 percent) used to calculate the central value of the social cost of carbon estimates is consistent with Circular A-4 guidance. Some working group participants told us that they recognized the importance of using OMB guidance, including Circular A-4, in developing the Technical Support Document. The Technical Support Document states that the working group decided

---

[26]The Stanford Energy Modeling Forum is an international forum for sharing and facilitating discussions on energy policy and global climate issues among researchers.

[27]Equilibrium climate sensitivity is the long-term increase in the annual global-average surface temperature from a sustained doubling of the concentration of carbon dioxide in the atmosphere relative to preindustrial levels of the concentration of carbon dioxide in the atmosphere.

to calculate estimates for several discount rates (2.5, 3, and 5 percent) because the academic literature shows that the social cost of carbon is highly sensitive to the discount rate chosen, and because no consensus exists on the appropriate rate. It further states that, in light of such uncertainties, the working group determined that these three discount rates reflect reasonable judgments about the appropriate rate to use. Several participants stated that the working group chose this approach to capture varied concerns and interests, including participants' respective knowledge of the academic literature, on selecting the discount rate.

Once the working group agreed on these modeling inputs, EPA officials supervised their use in running the models to calculate the social cost of carbon estimates. All other model assumptions and features were unchanged by the working group, which weighted each model equally to calculate the final estimates. Several participants stated that an important principle for the leaders of the working group was that the working group reach consensus on the modeling inputs before running the models and agree, in advance, to accept the results based on the inputs selected, whatever the outcome. Through this approach, the working group developed a set of four social cost of carbon estimates for use in regulatory impact analyses. The first three values are based on the average of the estimates produced by all three models and selected modeling inputs at the three discount rates chosen. The fourth value was included to represent higher-than-expected economic impacts from climate change, and it is based on an average of certain values produced by each model at a 3 percent discount rate.[28] To capture uncertainties involved in regulatory impact analysis, the Technical Support Document emphasizes the importance of agencies considering all four estimates when conducting analyses.

According to EPA documentation and several participants, groups from outside the federal government did not participate in the working group, but the working group used some outside resources, specifically technical assistance. As noted in the Technical Support Document, the working group explored technical literature in relevant fields for developing the social cost of carbon estimates. Members of the working group

---

[28]According to the Technical Support Document, the working group determined the fourth value by combining the values appearing at the furthest reaches of the distributions produced by each model. For this purpose, the working group used values produced from all three models for the 95th percentile at a 3 percent discount rate.

sometimes contacted researchers or developers of key data in an effort to ensure that the working group had a clear understanding of the information and how to use it. For example, according to several participants, members of the working group consulted with lead authors of a chapter on climate sensitivity that appears in the *Fourth Assessment Report of the Intergovernmental Panel on Climate Change*.[29] According to the Technical Support Document, after consulting with the chapter authors, the working group was able to make some decisions to assist with statistical analyses needed to develop the social cost of carbon estimates. Many participants stated that the working group also consulted with the developers of the models used by the group to develop the estimates. For example, EPA officials told us that, while they conducted runs for one model that was readily available to the public, they spent a few days training with the developer of a second model before using it to conduct runs. They also contracted with the developer of a third model to run the model according to the decisions reached by the working group. They stated that they ran all of the 2013 estimates themselves, but that they continued to consult with the model developers to do so.

According to many participants and the 2013 update to the Technical Support Document, the only changes made to the models used for the 2013 revisions were those that the model developers incorporated into the latest versions of the models and that were subsequently used in peer-reviewed academic literature. Specifically, the developers updated the academic models to reflect new scientific information, such as in sea level rise and associated damages, resulting in higher estimates.[30] The working group did not make changes in the modeling inputs that it used

---

[29]Intergovernmental Panel on Climate Change, *Climate Change 2007: The Physical Science Basis. Contribution of Working Group I to the Fourth Assessment Report of the Intergovernmental Panel on Climate Change* (S. Solomon, et al. [eds.])(Cambridge, UK: Cambridge University Press, 2007).

[30]This new scientific information included an explicit representation of sea level rise and associated damages, updated climate change adaptation assumptions, and updated damage functions for agricultural impacts.

for the 2010 estimates.[31] Several participants said that, while the original working group included frequent, hours-long meetings over several months, the working group assembled to discuss the 2013 revisions only met a few times. According to the 2010 Technical Support Document, the working group is committed to updating its estimates as the science and economic understanding of climate change and its impacts on society improve over time.

Took Steps to Disclose Limitations and Incorporate New Information

According to several participants and the Technical Support Document, the working group's processes and methods took steps to disclose limitations and incorporate new information by considering public comments and revising the estimates as updated economic and scientific research became available. The Technical Support Document discusses several limitations of its estimates and areas that the working group identified as being in particular need of additional exploration and research. For example, it points out that none of the three models accounts for damages from wildlife loss or ocean acidification caused by carbon dioxide emissions. Also, the models cannot completely predict how technology may adapt to warmer temperatures. In addition, according to the Technical Support Document, the models may not fully consider the effects of damages due to potential catastrophic events, such as the melting of Antarctic ice sheets. As a result of such limitations, the models may underestimate damages from increased carbon emissions, according to the Technical Support Document. The Technical Support Document states that, as a result of these limitations, the social cost of carbon estimates should continue to evolve as knowledge is gained, and available models improve. Some of the participating agencies have incorporated discussions of these limitations into regulatory impact analyses using social cost of carbon estimates. For example, in a 2012 rule setting pollution standards for certain power plants, EPA noted that

---

[31]In January 2014, a former coleader of the working group discussed some of the reasons behind this approach in a presentation before the annual meeting of the American Economic Association, a leading economic interest group. See Cass Sunstein, "On Not Revisiting Official Discount Rates: Institutional Inertia and the Social Cost of Carbon" (paper presented at the annual meeting of the American Economic Association, Philadelphia, PA, Jan. 3, 2014). In 2013, another former coleader of the working group published a paper detailing the working group's methodology. See Greenstone, Michael et al., "Developing a Social Cost of Carbon for U.S. Regulatory Analysis: A Methodology and Interpretation," *Review of Environmental Economics and Policy 7*, no. 1: 23-46 (2013).

the social cost of carbon estimates are subject to limitations and uncertainties.[32]

Over the years, there have been opportunities for public comment on the various individually developed and working group estimates of the social cost of carbon for regulatory impact analysis, and several participants stated that these estimates were developed with input from the public. Since 2008, agencies have published over three dozen regulatory actions for public comment in the *Federal Register* that use various social cost of carbon estimates in regulatory impact analyses. While some of them specifically sought comments on the development of the social cost of carbon estimates used, and others did not, these regulatory actions were open to public comment, in general, for approximately 60 days and, according to OMB staff and other participants, agencies received many comments on the estimates through this process. Several participants stated that, while they discussed such public comments during working group meetings, individual agencies typically do not coordinate formally with other agencies on their reviews of comments received. According to the Technical Support Document, the working group convened, in part, to consider public comments on issues related to the social cost of carbon. After considering public comments on the interim values that agencies used in several rules, the working group developed the Technical Support Document, according to these participants and to the Technical Support Document. Several participants told us that the working group decided to revise the estimates for the first time in 2013 after agencies received a number of public comments encouraging revisions because the models used to develop the 2010 estimates had been subsequently updated and used in peer-reviewed academic literature. OMB staff stated that this theme was reflected in several public comments on regulations using the 2010 estimates.

In November 2013, OMB published a request in the *Federal Register* for public comments on all aspects of the Technical Support Document and

---

[32]National Emission Standards for Hazardous Air Pollutants From Coal- and Oil-Fired Electric Utility Steam Generating Units and Standards of Performance for Fossil-Fuel-Fired Electric Utility, Industrial-Commercial-Institutional, and Small Industrial-Commercial-Institutional Steam Generating Units, 77 Fed. Reg. 9304 (Feb. 16, 2012).

its use of the models to develop estimates of the social cost of carbon.[33] The notice stated that OMB is particularly interested in comments on the selection of the models for use in developing the estimates, how the distribution of estimates should be represented in regulatory impact analyses, and the strengths and limitations of the overall approach. OMB staff told us that they decided to issue the request in response to calls for additional transparency, and that they received over 100 unique comments and thousands of identical form-letter comments in response to the request. They said that, since they were still reviewing the comments received, they had not yet decided on steps for responding to them, but that they expect to review them with the working group to determine whether they could inform future updates to the Technical Support Document. OMB staff stated that they have already made most of the comments publicly available online at http://www.regulations.gov/ and that all of the comments would be made available soon.

The Technical Support Document states that the working group would regularly revisit the social cost of carbon estimates as new information becomes available due to improved scientific and economic research. The Technical Support Document set a goal of revisiting the estimates within 2 years, or when substantially updated models become available. Many participants told us that, to revise the estimates in 2013, the working group met only a few times and mostly for participants from EPA to present information about updates made to the models since the group last met in 2010. The updates touched on a variety of issues, including how some models represent damages from sea level rise. The 2013 update to the Technical Support Document states that it acknowledges the continued limitations described in the original Technical Support Document, and that it updates the estimates based on new versions of the underlying models without revisiting the working group's decisions on modeling inputs. Several participants stated that they reviewed drafts of the 2013 update to the Technical Support Document, but that there was little new information to review because only the models had been updated. In addition to stating that the working group would regularly

---

[33]Technical Support Document: Technical Update of the Social Cost of Carbon for Regulatory Impact Analysis under Executive Order No. 12866, 78 Fed. Reg. 70,586 (Nov. 26, 2013). In January 2014, OMB extended the public comment period through February 26, 2014. *See* Technical Support Document: Technical Update of the Social Cost of Carbon for Regulatory Impact Analysis Under Executive Order No. 12866, 79 Fed. Reg. 4359 (Jan. 27, 2014).

revisit its estimates, the Technical Support Document states that the working group will continue to support research to improve the estimates and hopes to develop methods to value other greenhouse gases as part of its ongoing work.[34]

Agency Comments

We provided a draft of this report for review and comment to the Departments of Agriculture, Commerce, Energy, Transportation, and the Treasury; EPA; and OMB. Only the Department of the Treasury provided written comments, which we received on July 14, 2014, and are reproduced in appendix II; in its written comments, the Department of the Treasury stated that the draft report does a good job of capturing the interagency process through which the estimates of the social cost of carbon were developed. In oral comments provided on July 15, 2014, OMB staff confirmed that OMB generally agreed with the report findings. OMB staff also provided technical comments, which we incorporated into the report, as appropriate. The Department of Energy and EPA provided technical comments only, which we incorporated into the report, as appropriate. In e-mails received on July 1, July 9, and July 14, 2014, respectively, the liaisons from the Departments of Agriculture, Commerce, and Transportation stated that the departments did not have any comments on the draft report.

As agreed with your offices, unless you publicly announce the contents of this report earlier, we plan no further distribution until 30 days from the report date. At that time, we will send copies to the appropriate congressional committees; the Secretaries of Agriculture, Commerce, Energy, Transportation, and the Treasury; the Administrator of EPA; the

---

[34]In late 2010 and early 2011, EPA and the Department of Energy sponsored two workshops on valuing climate change damages for regulatory analysis. The agencies reported that they sponsored the workshops to prepare for and inform future working group activities. See ICF International, *Workshop Report: Improving the Assessment and Valuation of Climate Change Impacts for Policy and Regulatory Analysis – Part 1* (January 2011); summary of workshop sponsored by EPA and the Department of Energy and titled "Modeling Climate Change Impacts and Associated Economic Damages" (Washington, D.C.: Nov. 18-19, 2010) and *Workshop Report: Improving the Assessment and Valuation of Climate Change Impacts for Policy and Regulatory Analysis – Part 2* (March 2011); summary of workshop sponsored by EPA and the Department of Energy and titled "Research on Climate Change Impacts and Associated Economic Damages" (Washington, D.C., Jan. 27-28, 2011).

Director of OMB; and other interested parties. In addition, the report will be available at no charge on the GAO website at http://www.gao.gov.

If you or your staff members have any questions about this report, please contact me at (202) 512-3841 or gomezj@gao.gov. Contact points for our Offices of Congressional Relations and Public Affairs may be found on the last page of this report. Key contributors to this report are listed in appendix III.

J. Alfredo Gómez
Director, Natural Resources and Environment

Appendix I: Regulatory Actions, by Agency and Type of Social Cost of Carbon Estimates Used, 2008-2014

This appendix lists regulatory actions from 2008 to 2014 and the type of social cost of carbon estimates used (i.e., individually developed, interim, 2010, or 2013) in the actions' regulatory impact analyses. For each regulatory action, table 3 lists the date published in the *Federal Register*, the agency conducting the action, the name and status of the rule associated with the action, and the action's citation in the *Federal Register*.

Table 3: Regulatory Actions by Agency and Type of Social Cost of Carbon Estimates Used in the Regulatory Impact Analysis, 2008-2014

Date published in the *Federal Register*	Agency	Title	Status of rule	Federal Register citation
Individually developed agency estimates				
May 2, 2008	Department of Transportation (Transportation), National Highway Traffic Safety Administration (NHTSA)	Average Fuel Economy Standards, Passenger Cars and Light Trucks; Model Years 2011-2015	Proposed	73 Fed. Reg. 24,352
July 30, 2008	Environmental Protection Agency (EPA)	Regulating Greenhouse Gas Emissions Under the Clean Air Act	Advanced Notice of Proposed Rulemaking	73 Fed. Reg. 44,354
Aug. 25, 2008	Department of Energy (Energy)	Energy Conservation Program for Commercial and Industrial Equipment: Energy Conservation Standards for Commercial Ice-Cream Freezers; Self-Contained Commercial Refrigerators, Commercial Freezers, and Commercial Refrigerator-Freezers Without Doors; and Remote Condensing Commercial Refrigerators, Commercial Freezers, and Commercial Refrigerator-Freezers	Proposed	73 Fed. Reg. 50,072
Oct. 7, 2008	Energy	Energy Conservation Program for Commercial and Industrial Equipment: Packaged Terminal Air Conditioner and Packaged Terminal Heat Pump Energy Conservation Standards	Final	73 Fed. Reg. 58,772

Date published in the *Federal Register*	Agency	Title	Status of rule	*Federal Register* citation
Oct. 17, 2008	Energy	Energy Conservation Program: Energy Conservation Standards for Certain Consumer Products (Dishwashers, Dehumidifiers, Electric and Gas Kitchen Ranges and Ovens, and Microwave Ovens) and for Certain Commercial and Industrial Equipment (Commercial Clothes Washers)	Proposed	73 Fed. Reg. 62,034
Jan. 9, 2009	Energy	Energy Conservation Program for Commercial and Industrial Equipment: Energy Conservation Standards for Commercial Ice-Cream Freezers; Self-Contained Commercial Refrigerators, Commercial Freezers, and Commercial Refrigerator-Freezers Without Doors; and Remote Condensing Commercial Refrigerators, Commercial Freezers, and Commercial Refrigerator-Freezers	Final	74 Fed. Reg. 1092
Mar. 30, 2009	Transportation, NHTSA	Average Fuel Economy Standards Passenger Cars and Light Trucks Model Year 2011	Final	74 Fed. Reg. 14,196
Apr. 8, 2009	Energy	Energy Conservation Program: Energy Conservation Standards for Certain Consumer Products (Dishwashers, Dehumidifiers, Microwave Ovens, and Electric and Gas Kitchen Ranges and Ovens) and for Certain Commercial and Industrial Equipment (Commercial Clothes Washers)	Final	74 Fed. Reg. 16,040
Apr. 13, 2009	Energy	Energy Conservation Program: Energy Conservation Standards for General Service Fluorescent Lamps and Incandescent Reflector Lamps	Proposed	74 Fed. Reg. 16,920
May 26, 2009	EPA	Regulation of Fuels and Fuel Additives: Changes to Renewable Fuel Standard Program	Proposed	74 Fed. Reg. 24,904
May 29, 2009	Energy	Energy Conservation Program: Energy Conservation Standards for Refrigerated Bottled or Canned Beverage Vending Machines	Proposed	74 Fed. Reg. 26,020

Date published in the Federal Register	Agency	Title	Status of rule	Federal Register citation
July 14, 2009	Energy	Energy Conservation Program: Energy Conservation Standards and Test Procedures for General Service Fluorescent Lamps and Incandescent Reflector Lamps	Final	74 Fed. Reg. 34,080
July 22, 2009	Energy	Energy Conservation Program for Certain Industrial Equipment: Energy Conservation Standards and Test Procedures for Commercial Heating, Air-Conditioning, and Water-Heating Equipment	Final	74 Fed. Reg. 36,312

Interim governmentwide estimates

Date published in the Federal Register	Agency	Title	Status of rule	Federal Register citation
Aug. 31, 2009	Energy	Energy Conservation Program: Energy Conservation Standards for Refrigerated Bottled or Canned Beverage Vending Machines	Final	74 Fed. Reg. 44,914
Sep. 28, 2009	EPA and Transportation, NHTSA	Proposed Rulemaking to Establish Light-Duty Vehicle Greenhouse Gas Emission Standards and Corporate Average Fuel Economy Standards	Proposed	74 Fed. Reg. 49,454
Nov. 9, 2009	Energy	Energy Conservation Program: Energy Conservation Standards for Certain Consumer Products (Dishwashers, Dehumidifiers, Microwave Ovens, and Electric and Gas Kitchen Ranges and Ovens) and for Certain Commercial and Industrial Equipment (Commercial Clothes Washers)	Supplemental Notice of Proposed Rulemaking	74 Fed. Reg. 57,738
Nov. 24, 2009	Energy	Energy Conservation Program: Energy Conservation Standards for Small Electric Motors	Proposed	74 Fed. Reg. 61,410
Dec. 11, 2009	Energy	Energy Conservation Program: Energy Conservation Standards for Residential Water Heaters, Direct Heating Equipment, and Pool Heaters	Proposed	74 Fed. Reg. 65,852
Jan. 8, 2010	Energy	Energy Conservation Program: Energy Conservation Standards for Certain Consumer Products (Dishwashers, Dehumidifiers, Microwave Ovens, and Electric and Gas Kitchen Ranges and Ovens) and for Certain Commercial and Industrial Equipment (Commercial Clothes Washers)	Final	75 Fed. Reg. 1122

Date published in the *Federal Register*	Agency	Title	Status of rule	*Federal Register* citation
Mar. 26, 2010	EPA	Regulation of Fuels and Fuel Additives: Changes to Renewable Fuel Standard Program	Final	75 Fed. Reg. 14,670
June 21, 2010	EPA	Hazardous and Solid Waste Management System; Identification and Listing of Special Wastes; Disposal of Coal Combustion Residuals From Electric Utilities	Proposed	75 Fed. Reg. 35,128

2010 government-wide estimates

Date published in the *Federal Register*	Agency	Title	Status of rule	*Federal Register* citation
Mar. 9, 2010	Energy	Energy Conservation Program: Energy Conservation Standards for Small Electric Motors	Final	75 Fed. Reg. 10,874
Apr. 16, 2010	Energy	Energy Conservation Program: Energy Conservation Standards for Residential Water Heaters, Direct Heating Equipment, and Pool Heaters	Final	75 Fed. Reg. 20,112
May 7, 2010	EPA and Transportation, NHTSA	Light Duty Vehicle Greenhouse Gas Emission Standards and Corporate Average Fuel Economy Standards	Final	75 Fed. Reg. 25,324
May 28, 2010	Transportation, Federal Aviation Administration	Automatic Dependent Surveillance—Broadcast (ADS-B) Out Performance Requirements to Support Air Traffic Control (ATC) Service	Final	75 Fed. Reg. 30,160
Aug. 2, 2010	EPA	Federal Implementation Plans To Reduce Interstate Transport of Fine Particulate Matter and Ozone	Proposed	75 Fed. Reg. 45,210
Sep. 9, 2010	EPA	National Emission Standards for Hazardous Air Pollutants from the Portland Cement Manufacturing Industry and Standards of Performance for Portland Cement Plants	Final	75 Fed. Reg. 54,970
Oct. 14, 2010	EPA	Standards of Performance for New Stationary Sources and Emission Guidelines for Existing Sources: Sewage Sludge Incineration Units	Proposed	75 Fed. Reg. 63,260
Nov. 30, 2010	EPA and Transportation, NHTSA	Greenhouse Gas Emissions Standards and Fuel Efficiency Standards for Medium- and Heavy-Duty Engines and Vehicles	Proposed	75 Fed. Reg. 74,152

Date published in the _Federal Register_	Agency	Title	Status of rule	_Federal Register_ citation
Mar. 14, 2011	EPA	National Emission Standards for Hazardous Air Pollutants: Mercury Emissions from Mercury Cell Chlor-Alkali Plants	Supplemental Proposed Rule	76 Fed. Reg. 13,852
Mar. 21, 2011	EPA	Standards of Performance for New Stationary Sources and Emission Guidelines for Existing Sources: Sewage Sludge Incineration Units	Final	76 Fed. Reg. 15,372
Mar. 21, 2011	EPA	National Emission Standards for Hazardous Air Pollutants for Major Sources: Industrial, Commercial, and Institutional Boilers and Process Heaters	Final	76 Fed. Reg. 15,608
Apr. 11, 2011	Energy	Energy Conservation Program: Energy Conservation Standards for Fluorescent Lamp Ballasts	Proposed	76 Fed. Reg. 20,090
Apr. 21, 2011	Energy	Energy Conservation Program: Energy Conservation Standards for Residential Clothes Dryers and Room Air Conditioners	Direct Final	76 Fed. Reg. 22,454
June 27, 2011	Energy	Energy Conservation Program: Energy Conservation Standards for Residential Furnaces and Residential Central Air Conditioners and Heat Pumps	Direct Final	76 Fed. Reg. 37,408
Aug. 8, 2011	EPA	Federal Implementation Plans: Interstate Transport of Fine Particulate Matter and Ozone and Correction of SIP Approvals[a]	Final	76 Fed. Reg. 48,208
Sep. 15, 2011	EPA and Transportation, NHTSA	Greenhouse Gas Emissions Standards and Fuel Efficiency Standards for Medium- and Heavy-Duty Engines and Vehicles	Final	76 Fed. Reg. 57,106
Sep. 15, 2011	Energy	Energy Conservation Program: Energy Conservation Standards for Residential Refrigerators, Refrigerator-Freezers, and Freezers	Final	76 Fed. Reg. 57,516
Nov. 14, 2011	Energy	Energy Conservation Program: Energy Conservation Standards for Fluorescent Lamp Ballasts	Final	76 Fed. Reg. 70,548
Dec. 1, 2011	EPA and Transportation, NHTSA	2017 and Later Model Year Light-Duty Vehicle Greenhouse Gas Emissions and Corporate Average Fuel Economy Standards	Proposed	76 Fed. Reg. 74,854

Date published in the *Federal Register*	Agency	Title	Status of rule	*Federal Register* citation
Dec. 23, 2011	EPA	Commercial and Industrial Solid Waste Incineration Units: Reconsideration and Proposed Amendments; Non-Hazardous Secondary Materials That Are Solid Waste	Proposed	76 Fed. Reg. 80,452
Jan. 17, 2012	Energy	Energy Conservation Program for Certain Industrial Equipment: Energy Conservation Standards and Test Procedures for Commercial Heating, Air-Conditioning, and Water-Heating Equipment	Proposed	77 Fed. Reg. 2356
Feb. 10, 2012	Energy	Energy Conservation Program: Energy Conservation Standards for Distribution Transformers	Proposed	77 Fed. Reg. 7282
Feb. 14, 2012	Energy	Energy Conservation Program: Energy Conservation Standards for Standby Mode and Off Mode for Microwaves	Supplemental Notice of Proposed Rulemaking	77 Fed. Reg. 8526
Feb. 16, 2012	EPA	National Emission Standards for Hazardous Air Pollutants from Coal- and Oil-Fired Electric Utility Steam Generating Units and Standards of Performance for Fossil-Fuel-Fired Electric Utility, Industrial-Commercial-Institutional, and Small Industrial-Commercial-Institutional Steam Generating Units	Final	77 Fed. Reg. 9304
Mar. 27, 2012	Energy	Energy Conservation Program: Energy Conservation Standards for Battery Chargers and External Power Supplies	Proposed	77 Fed. Reg. 18,478
Apr. 13, 2012	EPA	Standards of Performance for Greenhouse Gas Emissions for New Stationary Sources: Electric Utility Generating Units	Proposed	77 Fed. Reg. 22,392
May 30, 2012	Energy	Energy Conservation Program: Energy Conservation Standards for Residential Dishwashers	Direct Final	77 Fed. Reg. 31,918
May 31, 2012	Energy	Energy Conservation Program: Energy Conservation Standards for Residential Clothes Washers	Direct Final	77 Fed. Reg. 32,308
Oct. 15, 2012	EPA and Transportation, NHTSA	2017 and Later Model Year Light-Duty Vehicle Greenhouse Gas Emissions and Corporate Average Fuel Economy Standards	Final	77 Fed. Reg. 62,624

Date published in the *Federal Register*	Agency	Rule	Status of rule	*Federal Register* citation
Apr. 18, 2013	Energy	Energy Conservation Program: Energy Conservation Standards for Distribution Transformers	Final	78 Fed. Reg. 23,336
June 7, 2013	EPA	Effluent Limitations Guidelines and Standards for the Steam Electric Power Generating Point Source Category	Proposed	78 Fed. Reg. 34,432

2013 revised governmentwide estimates

June 17, 2013	Energy	Energy Conservation Program: Energy Conservation Standards for Standby Mode and Off Mode for Microwave Ovens	Final	78 Fed. Reg. 36,316
Aug. 20, 2013	Energy	Energy Conservation Program: Energy Conservation Standards for Metal Halide Lamp Fixtures	Proposed	78 Fed. Reg. 51,464
Sep. 11, 2013	Energy	Energy Conservation Program: Energy Conservation Standards for Walk-In Coolers and Freezers	Proposed	78 Fed. Reg. 55,782
Sep. 11, 2013	Energy	Energy Conservation Program: Energy Conservation Standards for Commercial Refrigeration Equipment	Proposed	78 Fed. Reg. 55,890
Oct. 25, 2013	Energy	Energy Conservation Program for Consumer Products: Energy Conservation Standards for Residential Furnace Fans	Proposed	78 Fed. Reg. 64,068
Dec. 6, 2013	Energy	Energy Conservation Program: Energy Conservation Standards for Commercial and Industrial Electric Motors	Proposed	78 Fed. Reg. 73,590
Jan. 8, 2014	EPA	Standards of Performance for Greenhouse Gas Emissions from New Stationary Sources: Electric Utility Generating Units	Proposed	79 Fed. Reg. 1430
Feb. 10, 2014	Energy	Energy Conservation Program: Energy Conservation Standards for Metal Halide Lamp Fixtures	Final	79 Fed. Reg. 7746
Feb. 10, 2014	Energy	Energy Conservation Program: Energy Conservation Standards for External Power Supplies	Final	79 Fed. Reg. 7846
Mar. 4, 2014	Energy	Energy Conservation Program: Energy Conservation Standards for Commercial Clothes Washers	Proposed	79 Fed. Reg. 12,302

Date published in the *Federal Register*	Agency	Rule	Status of rule	*Federal Register* citation
Mar. 17, 2014	Energy	Energy Conservation Program: Energy Conservation Standards for Automatic Commercial Ice Makers	Proposed	79 Fed. Reg. 14,846
Mar. 28, 2014	Energy	Energy Conservation Program: Energy Conservation Standards for Commercial Refrigeration Equipment	Final	79 Fed. Reg. 17,726
Apr. 29, 2014	Energy	Energy Conservation Program: Energy Conservation Standards for General Service Fluorescent Lamps and Incandescent Reflector Lamps	Proposed	79 Fed. Reg. 24,068
May 29, 2014	Energy	Energy Conservation Program: Energy Conservation Standards for Commercial and Industrial Electric Motors	Final	79 Fed. Reg. 30,934
June 3, 2014	Energy	Energy Conservation Program: Energy Conservation Standards for Walk-In Coolers and Freezers	Final	79 Fed. Reg. 32,050
June 18, 2014	EPA	Carbon Pollution Emission Guidelines for Existing Stationary Sources: Electric Utility Generating Units	Proposed	79 Fed. Reg. 34,830

Sources: Environmental Protection Agency and *Federal Register*. | GAO-14-663

Notes:

Regulatory actions in this table are as of June 18, 2014.

In 2008 and early 2009, individual estimates of the social cost of carbon were developed by each agency and typically based on estimates published in academic literature. The interim governmentwide estimates were developed in early 2009 by the Interagency Working Group on Social Cost of Carbon and derived from an average of selected estimates published in academic literature. The 2010 governmentwide estimates were developed by the Interagency Working Group on Social Cost of Carbon and issued in its February 2010 Technical Support Document. The 2013 revised governmentwide estimates were developed by the Interagency Working Group on Social Cost of Carbon and issued in a May 2013 update to the Technical Support Document, which was reissued with minor technical corrections in November 2013.

[a]SIP refers to State Implementation Plan.

Appendix II: Comments from the Department of the Treasury

DEPARTMENT OF THE TREASURY
WASHINGTON, D.C.

JUL 1 4 2014

TO: Director J. Alfredo Gomez, Government Accountability Office

FROM: Leonardo Martinez-Diaz, Deputy Assistant Secretary for Energy and
        Environment

RE: Draft report on Development of Social Cost of Carbon Estimate (361544)

Dear Director Gomez,

Thank you for the opportunity to review the draft report on the Development of the Social Cost
of Carbon Estimates (361544). The report does a good job of capturing the interagency process
through which the estimates of the social cost of carbon were developed. We have no further
comments on the draft.

Sincerely,

Leonardo Martinez-Diaz

Appendix III: GAO Contact and Staff Acknowledgments

GAO Contact	J. Alfredo Gómez, (202) 512-3841, or gomezj@gao.gov
Staff Acknowledgments	In addition to the individual named above, Janet Frisch (Assistant Director), Elizabeth Beardsley, Stephanie Gaines, Cindy Gilbert, Chad M. Gorman, Tim Guinane, Patricia Moye, Susan Offutt, Alison O'Neill, and Kiki Theodoropoulos made key contributions to this report.

GAO's Mission	The Government Accountability Office, the audit, evaluation, and investigative arm of Congress, exists to support Congress in meeting its constitutional responsibilities and to help improve the performance and accountability of the federal government for the American people. GAO examines the use of public funds; evaluates federal programs and policies; and provides analyses, recommendations, and other assistance to help Congress make informed oversight, policy, and funding decisions. GAO's commitment to good government is reflected in its core values of accountability, integrity, and reliability.
Obtaining Copies of GAO Reports and Testimony	The fastest and easiest way to obtain copies of GAO documents at no cost is through GAO's website (http://www.gao.gov). Each weekday afternoon, GAO posts on its website newly released reports, testimony, and correspondence. To have GAO e-mail you a list of newly posted products, go to http://www.gao.gov and select "E-mail Updates."
Order by Phone	The price of each GAO publication reflects GAO's actual cost of production and distribution and depends on the number of pages in the publication and whether the publication is printed in color or black and white. Pricing and ordering information is posted on GAO's website, http://www.gao.gov/ordering.htm. Place orders by calling (202) 512-6000, toll free (866) 801-7077, or TDD (202) 512-2537. Orders may be paid for using American Express, Discover Card, MasterCard, Visa, check, or money order. Call for additional information.
Connect with GAO	Connect with GAO on Facebook, Flickr, Twitter, and YouTube. Subscribe to our RSS Feeds or E-mail Updates. Listen to our Podcasts. Visit GAO on the web at www.gao.gov.
To Report Fraud, Waste, and Abuse in Federal Programs	Contact: Website: http://www.gao.gov/fraudnet/fraudnet.htm E-mail: fraudnet@gao.gov Automated answering system: (800) 424-5454 or (202) 512-7470
Congressional Relations	Katherine Siggerud, Managing Director, siggerudk@gao.gov, (202) 512-4400, U.S. Government Accountability Office, 441 G Street NW, Room 7125, Washington, DC 20548
Public Affairs	Chuck Young, Managing Director, youngc1@gao.gov, (202) 512-4800 U.S. Government Accountability Office, 441 G Street NW, Room 7149 Washington, DC 20548